IMAGES
of America

BROWN COUNTY

On the cover: The *Proctor K. Smiley* was a ferry that operated between Ripley and South Ripley, Kentucky, where the Chesapeake and Ohio Railroad trains stopped. It began service in the early 1880s, and various ferryboats operated from Ripley until 1951, the year before the Chesapeake and Ohio Railroad stopped service to South Ripley. (Courtesy of the Cincinnati Historical Society.)

IMAGES
of America

BROWN COUNTY

Greg and Lisa Haitz

ARCADIA
PUBLISHING

Published by Arcadia Publishing
Charleston, South Carolina

Library of Congress Catalog Card Number: 2006930905

For all general information contact Arcadia Publishing at:
Telephone 843-853-2070
Fax 843-853-0044
E-mail sales@arcadiapublishing.com
For customer service and orders:
Toll-Free 1-888-313-2665

Visit us on the Internet at www.arcadiapublishing.com

We dedicate this book to our parents, Albert and Mary Louise Haitz, and Dr. Marcel and Joyce Pons, our first and best teachers. We love you.

CONTENTS

ACKNOWLEDGMENTS

We would like to thank the following for their help with this work in providing information and/or photographs: Alison Gibson, director of the Union Township Public Library; Lee Edwards, curator of the Ripley Museum; Kay Haag of the Aberdeen-Huntington Township Museum; Dr. Ned Lodwick, president of the Brown County Historical Society; Al Rhonemus, past president of the Brown County Historical Society; Edie and Eddie Fath of the Ohio Tobacco Museum; Kay Fry of the Decatur/Byrd Township Museum; Lucille Gelter and Teresa Montgomery of the Russellville Museum; The Mount Orab Library; Kentucky Gateway Museum Center (Maysville); Cincinnati Public Library Rare Photographs; Cincinnati Historical Society; Bob and Betty Campbell; Cindi McIntosh; Tom White; Phil White; Judy Herman; Judith Richards Gray; Myrtle West; Wanda and Harry Donald; John Cooper; Dolores Stuhlreyer; Robert Russell; Shirley Moran; Bob Rapier; Mike Farris; Jeff Case; Jackie Hanson; Angie Bridges; Gladys Lucas; Caroline Miller; Mary Jane Maston; Erma Spiller; and David Gray.

Alison Gibson and Dr. Ned Lodwick helped us with proofreading, for which we are very grateful. Thanks to our editor at Arcadia, Melissa Basilone, for being so patient with first time authors. Any mistakes in this work are our own.

INTRODUCTION

History cannot give us a program for the future, but it can give us a fuller understanding of ourselves, and of our common humanity, so that we can better face the future.

—Robert Penn Warren

The fertile land that was to become Brown County was inhabited by various Native American tribes, including the Miami, Wyandot, Shawnee, Delaware, and Mingo (Iroquois), who hunted and trapped on this land.

The county was created from parts of Adams and Clermont Counties by the Ohio legislature in 1818 and named in honor of Gen. Jacob Brown, a war hero of the War of 1812.

The early settlers were from many different countries and brought with them strong agricultural traditions and skills. The growing of tobacco was one such tradition that became vital to Brown County's growth, and, until recently, it was the county's chief export. The German settlers brought with them expertise in wine making. There were many small vineyards in the Ohio Valley until the Civil War took workers away from their land and disease killed many of the grapes.

For many years in its early history, one of the county's chief resources was horses. Draft horses from Brown County were shipped from the river towns to destinations up and down the Ohio and Mississippi Rivers in steamboats. The Ripley Horse Fair was held regularly on the last Saturday of each month. The horses of Brown County were considered some of the finest to be found.

Perhaps the most important asset for Brown County was, and is now, the Ohio River. Because it flowed west, the river was a main route for the expansion of the young United States. The name "Ohio" comes from the Native American word meaning "beautiful river."

The river opened Brown County's resources to the growing United States, enabling the citizens to send and receive trade goods from Pittsburgh, St. Louis, and New Orleans. Produce, livestock, and more were traded. The river also provided employment: Levanna and Ripley had shipyards that built many steamboats, including the *Argand*.

The towns along the river, however, were very different than they are today. The railroad expansion, as well as the advent of the automobile, slowed the growth of Brown County's river towns. They had many stores and shops that now can only be found in large cities. For example, today Higginsport has a population of about 200, with two restaurants and a bank; but in 1880, it had five general stores, two drugstores, two tin shops, one hardware store, a clothing store, five practicing physicians, and 10 tobacco warehouses.

During the 18th century, the Ohio River was also the southern boundary of the Northwest Territory, serving as the border between free and slave states. Thus, today Brown County is perhaps best known for its work before the Civil War on the Underground Railroad. The term "Underground Railroad" originated here, and people like John Rankin, John P. Parker, and many others worked to help free slaves from bondage and oppression, often at great personal sacrifice.

As in many parts of the country, the county too was also torn by the Civil War. Its most famous citizen, Ulysses S. Grant, president and the last commander of the Union Army, noted that "the line between the Rebel and Union element in Georgetown was so marked that it led to divisions even in churches." And yet, this "remarkable village," as Grant called it, "furnished the Union Army four general officers and one colonel, West Point graduates, and nine generals and field officers of Volunteers."

Like many small towns all over America, the people of Brown County had baseball teams, town bands, and places to go and relax for a day. In times of war, when our nation called, Brown County answered with men like Charles Young, the third African American to graduate from West Point.

Today Brown County is a bedroom community for Cincinnati, approximately 50 miles to the west, with many living in the peace and quiet of the country while working in the city. The main source of revenue is derived from tourism, with thousands coming every summer to go boating on the river, walk the steps of the Underground Railroad, or see where a president lived during his childhood.

The intention of the authors in writing this book was to share some of the rich history of Brown County and to bring forth some of the famous and not so famous residents who left their marks not only in the county but on the rest of the world. Their contributions should not be forgotten.

This book in no way represents a full history or Brown County. We limited the time period covered to 1818–1968, as well as the type of images, trying to use only images from that period. As a result, some interesting stories were left out, which we regret.

The citizens of Brown County are especially proud of their history. They open their doors to all who come to study the county's role in American history, and they devote their time to preserving the legacy of their ancestors and fellow citizens. We are proud to be their neighbors.

One

EARLY HISTORY

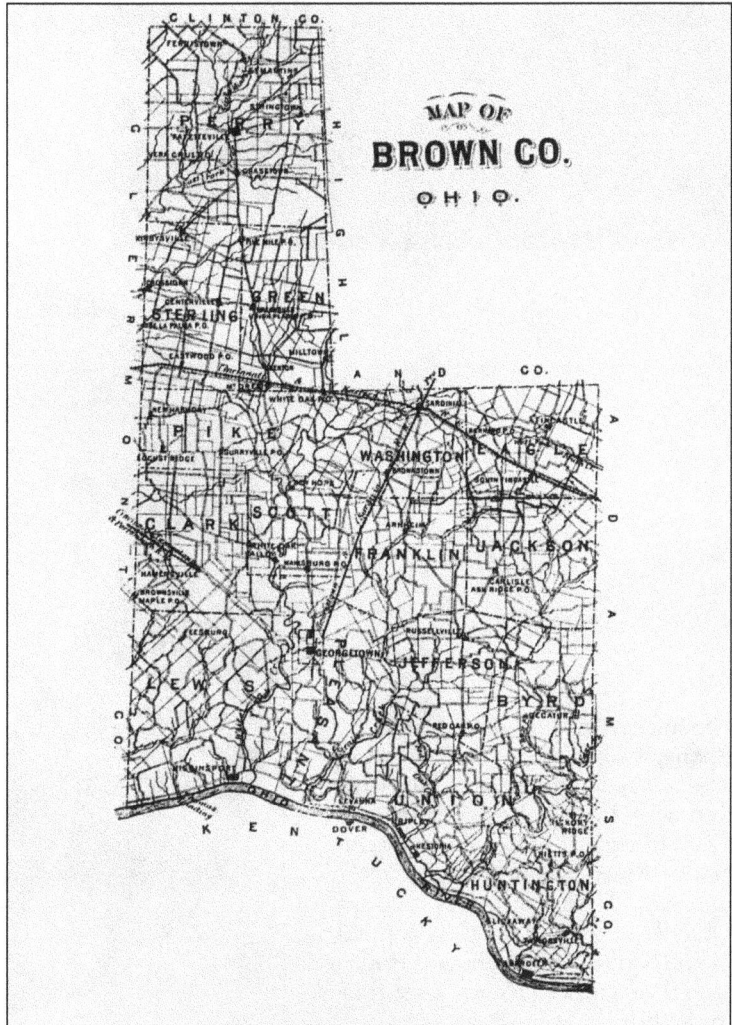

MAP OF
BROWN CO.
OHIO.

Brown County was created in 1818 by the Ohio legislature using areas of land taken from both Adams and Clermont Counties. The county was named for Gen. Jacob Brown, who was a commanding officer at the Battle of Lundy's Lane in Canada during the War of 1812. His successes in the Northwest made him a national hero. Brown County, Indiana, and Brown County, Illinois, were also named in his honor.

Daniel Boone, one of the most famous explorers in American history, was well acquainted with Brown County. In March 1787, near what is now Aberdeen, Boone, Simon Kenton, and others held a prisoner exchange on the Ohio River with Native Americans who were lead by the infamous Bluejacket. With the Native Americans on the Ohio side and the whites in Kentucky, captured Native Americans were exchanged for captured whites, and then a party was held to celebrate the agreement.

Simon Kenton, a friend of Daniel Boone, was a scout and frontiersman who traveled into Brown County from Kentucky. In 1778, Kenton went on a raid to recover horses stolen by the Native Americans near Eagle Creek in Ripley. While waiting for a stormy Ohio River to calm, he was captured by the Native Americans and made to "run the gauntlet." He was later traded to the British, from whom he escaped.

The oldest house currently standing in Brown County was built in 1793 by William Dixon and Cornelius Washburn on Eagle Creek at Logan's Gap. The two were scouts for the government and were sent to watch for Native Americans who were attacking settlers traveling down the Ohio River on their flatboats. This photograph was taken at the Brown County Fairgrounds, where the Dixon-Washburn Log House was moved after its preservation.

A monument erected by the Ripley chapter of the Daughters of the American Revolution was dedicated in 1914 and is shown in this old photograph. It commemorates Belteshazzar Dragoo and his family, who were the first permanent settlers in Brown County in 1794. The monument still stands next to Scofield Road close to Eagle Creek just outside of Ripley. Many Dragoo descendants still live in Brown County.

Residence of James Poage,—Ripley,.

Col. James Poage, who founded Ripley in 1804, lived in this lovely house. Granted a 1000-acre tract as a reward for his service in the Revolutionary War and his work as a surveyor, the new village was at first a few scattered cabins called Buttsville, then Staunton, and finally Ripley, after Gen. Eleazer Wheelock Ripley, famous after the War of 1812. Poage's son Robert helped the sons of John Rankin escort slaves along the Underground Railroad. The 1876 *Brown County Atlas* recorded the village of Ripley as having eight dry goods stores, 15 groceries, two hardware stores, three stove stores, two bookstores, three clothing stores, two hat stores, five boot and shoe stores, three jewelers, four merchant tailors, one newspaper, one telegraph, one express office, three livery stables, three hotels, one foundry, one piano factory, six tobacco warehouses, two breweries, one "establishment for the manufacture of unfermented wine," seven physicians, and seven lawyers.

Russell Shaw was born in Rensselaer County, New York. In 1802, he moved to the Brown County area, and after fighting in the War of 1812, in 1816 he laid out the town that now bears his name: Russellville. In 1817, 36 lots were offered for sale in Russellville, and all were sold within a short time.

The Shaw family home is shown in this photograph from 1890. It still stands today in Russellville at the corner of West Main and Kendall Streets.

In 1850, Daniel Keethler set up a town on the east bank of the Sterling Fork of White Oak Creek. He named this village Mount Oreb, taking the name from the Bible, although the spelling was later changed to its current Mount Orab. The village became a town in 1880. Pictured here is the Keethler Building in the center of Mount Orab.

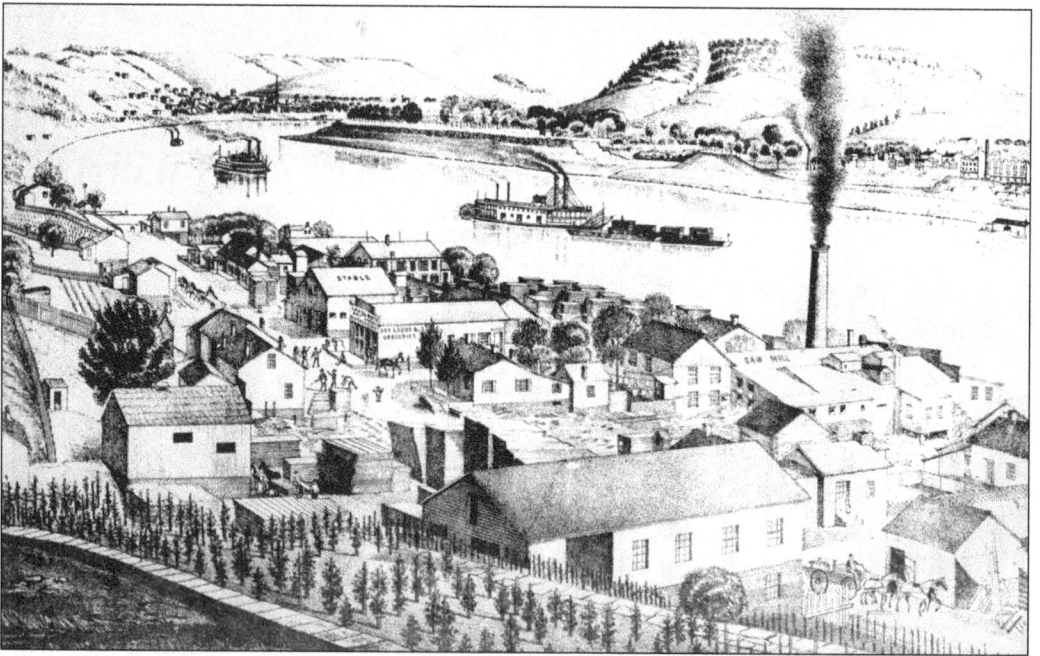

This is an early print of Levanna, which was a very prosperous town at one time, boasting a lumberyard, boatyard, and many homes. A fire in 1887 destroyed 21 buildings, including homes and the boat- and lumberyards. Fire departments from Ripley and Dover, Kentucky, sent their fire engines by ferryboat to help fight the blaze. The damage at the time was estimated at $100,000.

Ripley's first doctor, Alexander Campbell, was a merchant and antislavery leader who moved to Ohio in 1803 after freeing his slaves in Virginia. He was one of the first U.S. senators for Ohio from 1809 to 1813, leaving Washington, D.C., after it was burned by the British during the War of 1812. It is said that in Washington, he witnessed the trial run of Robert Fulton's steamboat.

Alexander Campbell's home is shown in this later photograph. The parlor of his home often served as the first courthouse for Brown County. This photograph is undated, although it is said to show a former slave who escaped to Ripley sitting on the front stairs of the home. At the time of the photograph, the former slave was said to be 107 years old. The pillars were added to this home in the 1930s, so the story could be true.

One of four generations of doctors, Dr. Thomas B. Wylie was the son of Dr. Adam Wylie of Ripley. Dr. Thomas B. Wylie was a graduate of Transylvania College in Lexington, Kentucky. He began his practice in New Orleans, then Natchez, Mississippi, before moving back to Brown County to practice first in Decatur and finally Ripley. He died in 1864, and his son Dr. Jefferson L. Wylie took over his practice followed by his son Dr. Alexander Wylie.

The Old Ripley Cemetery was the cemetery for the village from 1818 until the eve of the Civil War. Located just off Main Street next to Red Oak Creek, many of Ripley's early settlers are buried there, including its founder, Col. James Poage. Today visitors are amazed at the large tree that has grown up in the cemetery between four graves. Some of the headstones are now embedded into the tree.

This illustration from the 1876 *Brown County Atlas* shows the residence of Scott Kinkead. William Sr. and Eleanor Kinkead were originally from Virginia. Native Americans kidnapped Eleanor in 1763 and took her to their village called Chillicothe. She was held there for two years, finally escaping and returning to Virginia. The family had 12 children (two of whom were captured by Native Americans; one was born while Eleanor was held captive) and moved from Virginia to Versailles, Kentucky. Their son William Kinkead Jr. finally left Kentucky as he grew increasingly dissatisfied with the state's slavery laws. William Jr. and his wife, Annie, bought 300 acres in Brown County for $4.00 an acre and had nine children; Scott was their youngest child. Today the Kinkead Farm serves as the vineyards for the Kinkead Winery, makers of award-winning wine produced in Brown County and sold nationwide.

Every year, Aberdeen's Gretna Green Festival commemorates John Shelton and Massie "Squire" Beasley, who, like the magistrates of Gretna Green, Scotland, performed marriages without the formality of a license and often without the formality of parental consent. Beasley, pictured here, is believed to have married 7,228 couples from 1870 to 1892.

Sarah Boone Brooks Montgomery was the niece of Daniel Boone. Born in 1763, she was one of the water carriers during the siege of Bryan's Station, Kentucky, in 1782. She was married to Thomas Brooks until his death in 1800 and then to David Montgomery. The Montgomerys were some of the first settlers of Decatur in Brown County. Pictured here are some of their descendants at a family reunion.

On July 27, 1828, Ripley received one of the leading politicians of the 19th century, Henry Clay. The former congressman from Kentucky was then serving as secretary of state under Pres. John Quincy Adams. On the night of Clay's arrival, all of Ripley was illuminated by bonfires, and a salute was fired in his honor. Clay was then shown to the residence of Dr. Alexander Campbell, an old friend and former colleague in Congress.

During the presidential campaign of 1840, candidate William Henry Harrison made a stop in Ripley. Over 30,000 people crowded the banks of the Ohio River to hear "Old Tippecanoe" speak. Free food and cider were enjoyed by all at a great barbecue held after Harrison's speech.

Thomas L. Hamer, as U.S. congressman from Georgetown, was the man who recommended Ulysses S. Grant for West Point. In fact, when Congressman Hamer submitted Grant's name for admission, he wrote down the name Ulysses Simpson Grant, despite the fact that Grant's name was Hiram Ulysses Grant. Hamer thought Simpson was Grant's middle name because Simpson was his mother's maiden name. In order to attend West Point, Grant kept the name Ulysses Simpson Grant, and the rest, as they say, is history. Hamer died of yellow fever during the Mexican-American War. The photograph on the right is a ceremony of dedication of a monument to honor Hamer, which was on the courthouse square in Georgetown. It was later moved to the cemetery by the fairgrounds. Hamer was involved in an infamous incident involving abolitionists in Ohio in 1838. John B. Mahan, a noted abolitionist, was taken by force from Ohio to Kentucky for the crime of helping slaves escape. Mahan requested a routine writ of habeas corpus, which Hamer denied, as he was firmly pro-slavery at the time.

As an adult seeking his fortune, Jesse Grant moved his young family to the growing town of Georgetown, where he opened a tannery in 1823. He hoped that his son Ulysses, as he was known, would take over the business for him someday. Ulysses, however, hated the tannery business and eventually found a career elsewhere. Besides running his tannery, Jesse Grant also was involved in politics, a "solid Whig," as his son would call him, at one time serving as postmaster and later mayor of Georgetown. He was a close friend of Thomas L. Hamer; they were both members of the same debating society in Georgetown, but at one point, they had a falling out over politics. Hamer putting Jesse's son Ulysses's name in for recommendation to attend West Point ended their disagreement.

Born at Point Pleasant in Clermont County, Hiram Ulysses Grant moved to Georgetown at the age of one. He lived in Georgetown longer than anywhere else for the rest of his life. He loved horses and to work the land his family owned, about 50 acres outside of town. Unlike other young boys of the time, Grant did not like to go hunting. He was very fond of all animals. His father often hired out the young boy to drive people to Cincinnati in their wagon, which Grant gladly did to get away from the tannery. In his memoirs, Grant remembered his time in Georgetown as "fishing, going to the creek a mile away to swim in summer, taking a horse and visiting my grandparents in the adjoining county, fifteen miles off, skating on the ice in winter, or taking a horse and sleigh when there was snow on the ground."

Built in 1823, this home in Georgetown is where Ulysses S. Grant lived with his parents and four siblings until 1839, when he left for West Point. Standing at the corner of Water Street and Grant Avenue, the house was located across from the tannery operated by his family. In the upper right corner of this photograph, note the original cupola of the Brown County Courthouse, which was completed after Grant's time in Georgetown.

This is a front-side view of the Grant family home, taken in the early 20th century. The front porch was added after the Grants left Georgetown. Owned today by the Ohio Historical Society, the house has been recently renovated, and now an animatronic Ulysses S. Grant tells stories of his boyhood in Georgetown.

Another view of the Grant home, on the left, shows its location relative to the tannery operated by Ulysses S. Grant's father, in the foreground. His father, Jesse, noted that Ulysses would "rather do anything else under the sun than work in the tannery." Because of the smell and the blood he remembered from the tannery, at meal times Ulysses had his beef prepared well-done or even burnt for the rest of his life.

This photograph of the Grant tannery was taken well after Ulysses S. Grant's time in Georgetown. The wagon shown was owned by the Grant family and was used to carry wood and bark.

Grant attended school in this building in the 1830s in Georgetown, although this photograph shows it in the 1950s. Today the white paint has been removed, and the building has been restored to its original brick appearance. Located on South Water Street in Georgetown, the Grant School House is now operated by the Ohio Historical Society and the U. S. Grant Homestead Association. In his memoirs, Grant wrote of his time here:

The rod was freely used there, and I was not exempt from its influence. I can see John D. White—the school teacher—now, with his long beech switch always in his hand. It was not always the same one, either. Switches were brought in bundles, from a beech wood near the school house, by the boys for whose benefit they were intended. Often a whole bundle would be used up in a single day. I never had any hard feelings against my teacher, either while attending the school, or in later years when reflecting upon my experience. Mr. White was a kindhearted man, and was much respected by the community in which he lived.

There have been at least two recorded duels in Brown County, both involving Kentuckians. In 1812, Maj. Thomas Marshall (upper left) and Col. Charles S. Mitchell fought in Aberdeen across from Maysville. The outcome was not recorded. In another duel, a Confederate and former mayor of Maysville, Kentucky, William T. Casto (lower right) and Thomas Metcalfe, the son of a Kentucky governor and a colonel in the Union Army, fought a duel. Casto challenged Metcalfe after having been released from prison after an arrest by Metcalfe. Some say that the duel took place at Dover, Kentucky, just across the Ohio River from Brown County; others say it occurred on the Ohio side across from Dover. Interestingly, the two men used rifles. The shots were fired, with Casto missing his target. Metcalfe did not, and within a few minutes, Casto was dead.

Two

Underground Railroad and the Civil War

100 DOLLARS

REWARD!

Ranaway from the subscriber on the 27th of July, my Black Woman, named

EMILY,

Seventeen years of age, well grown, black color, has a whining voice. She took with her one dark calico and one blue and white dress, a red corded gingham bonnet; a white striped shawl and slippers. I will pay the above reward if taken near the Ohio river on the Kentucky side, or **THREE HUNDRED DOLLARS,** if taken in the State of Ohio, and delivered to me near Lewisburg, Mason County, Ky.   **THO'S. H. WILLIAMS.**

The Fugitive Slave Law of 1850 made any federal marshal or other official who did not arrest an alleged runaway slave liable to a fine of $1,000. The suspected slave could not ask for a jury trial or testify on his or her own behalf. In addition, any person aiding a runaway slave by providing food or shelter was subject to a six-month imprisonment and a $1,000 fine. This runaway slave poster from August 1853 is typical of just one of the methods used to catch runaway slaves. With Brown County just across the Ohio River from the slave state of Kentucky, the area became important to the abolitionist movement and the Underground Railroad. In fact, the term Underground Railroad comes from an incident in Brown County. A slave named Tice disappeared around Ripley so fast after crossing the Ohio River that his master, though in hot pursuit, said he "must have disappeared on an Underground Railroad."

John Rankin was the most important figure in the abolitionist movement in Brown County. A Presbyterian minister, he was asked to consider leaving the state of Tennessee, where he was preaching, as his sermons against slavery were considered too controversial in that part of the country. Rankin and his family then moved to Kentucky for a time, before making their way, in early 1822, to the free state of Ohio, crossing the Ohio River in a skiff. Rankin was fairly well known in the area for his abolitionist views, and by moving to Ripley, he was jeered at by some townspeople who sometimes beat tins outside his house while the family prayed inside. Rankin would not be moved, however, and let it be known his family was there to stay by building a three-section house on Front Street in Ripley, of which the other two parts were rented, before finally moving to Liberty Hill in 1829. Rankin preached his sermons from the Presbyterian church in Ripley, at one time saying, "the skin is but the dress God has thrown over the human frame."

This photograph shows the Rankin House, called the "Grand Central Station of the Underground Railroad," before restoration. This house was often the first stop on the network of stations in Brown County, with the next stops being Red Oak, then Decatur. Jean Rankin fed and clothed the slaves, and the Rankin children sometimes drove wagons and otherwise helped the slaves get to the next stop on their journey.

In all, the Rankin family is credited with helping over 2,000 slaves escape to freedom, none of whom were ever caught. Owned and operated by the Ohio Historical Society since 1948, the Rankin home is open to visitors. This picture was taken after the restoration.

The 100 steps that lead from Fourth Street in Ripley to the top of Liberty Hill and the Rankin House were called the Freedom Stairs. The Rankins kept the hillside cleared, so as to see any enemies who might approach the house. Many of the old steps were replaced in 1995.

The Rankin farm, with a beautiful vista of the Ohio River and Ripley some 500 feet below, was the perfect spot for the abolitionist family. Runaway slaves on the Kentucky shore knew to look for a lantern light, lit by the Rankins, to indicate that it was safe to cross the river and climb the hill to safety.

Awakened by his father at night, John Rankin Jr. would later recall that "I had answered that call too many times not to know what it meant. Fugitive slaves were downstairs. Ahead of us was a long walk in the dead of night under a cold winters' sky followed by the long cold walk back home, which must be made before daybreak."

The interior photographs shown on this page were taken in the 1960s. Once again, the Ohio Historical Society is redoing the house, and some interior modifications may be made, based on paint analysis done at the site.

Harriet Beecher Stowe is the author of *Uncle Tom's Cabin*, published in 1852. In her best-selling novel, one of the most famous stories is the escape of Eliza and her baby crossing the frozen ice to freedom. In fact, Stowe heard the story of a slave crossing the Ohio River with a baby from John Rankin. The Stowe family was active in the abolitionist movement in Cincinnati, and Stowe's husband taught at the Lane Seminary in Cincinnati. Rankin had a son at the same seminary, and this might have been where Rankin told the story of Eliza to Stowe, although there were many other opportunities. Stowe never divulged where she heard the story, as John Rankin could have been heavily fined and imprisoned if it were known that the story originated with him.

ELIZA'S ESCAPE OVER THE OHIO RIVER.

Although some details of the story vary, there can be no doubt that Eliza crossed the partially frozen Ohio River carrying her small child and a board in case she fell into the freezing water. Making her way to the shore after falling in three times, she finally arrived at the Rankin home, where she sat before a fire and was given new clothes. John Rankin Jr. later recalled that "so far as we were concerned, it was only another incident of many a similar character. It is strange how this fugitive mother figured into the history of our country. She had no name, no monument erected to her. We two boys had helped her make history, and were deaf, dumb, and blind to its significance." Three years later, a smallish woman approached the Rankin farm wearing men's clothing—it was the slave, Eliza. She had returned with a Canadian man, whom she was paying, to free her daughter and grandchildren from a slave house in Dover, Kentucky.

"Eliza of Uncle Tom's Cabin Fame and her Child escaped from this house to the Ohio Shore on the Floating Ice."

Eliza House, South Ripley, Ky.
Published by Maddox Drug Co., Ripley, Ohio.

Through exploits worthy of an adventure novel, an escape began. Eliza and a Canadian man got the slaves to the Kentucky shore, where they hid for a day in the thick brush. One grandchild, a house slave, could not be saved, as she could not be safely contacted with the details of the escape. Later that night, the fugitives were silently rowed across the darkened river. With the help of Ripley townspeople, including the McGagues, Rankins, and others, the group made its way through Brown County to Hillsboro, then eventually to Canada. Published by the Maddox Drug Company, Ripley, this unique postcard purportedly shows the house, located in Dover, Kentucky, where the escape took place.

John and Jean Rankin are pictured here on their 50th anniversary in 1866. The Rankin family, John Rankin and Jean Rankin (née Lowry) and their 13 children, all worked to help fleeing slaves escape to freedom from their home on Liberty Hill. Through times of financial hardships and threats of violence, arson, and more, the Rankins and their fellow abolitionists kept up the fight against slavery. The entire family is represented, although in an unusual way; two missing family members have been added into the photograph by the photographer. The Rankins moved from their home on the hill, living with children in their later years. In the book *Beyond the River*, Ann Hagedorn writes of Henry Ward Beecher being asked, "Who abolished slavery?" His response was "John Rankin and his sons did it."

By 1960, when this photograph was taken, this home had fallen into disrepair, belying its long and storied history as the home of John P. Parker. One of the more fascinating and inspiring individuals in the Ohio abolitionist movement, Parker had been born to a slave in Virginia and was sold into slavery. He was taught to read and write by the sons of one of his masters. He later was sold and permitted to work in a foundry, where he learned that trade. After 18 months, he had saved enough money to purchase his freedom, moving to Cincinnati and then eventually to Ripley. Parker and his partner William Hood purchased a foundry in 1865, naming it the Phoenix Foundry, and by the 1890s, it was the largest business of its kind between Cincinnati and Portsmouth, Ohio.

In addition to running his successful foundry, Parker helped many slaves who came across the Ohio River to his house adjoining the Phoenix Foundry. He said his hatred of slavery was not due to the physical degradation but rather "the taking away from a human being the initiative, of thinking, of doing his own ways." By his own account, he helped more than 400 slaves to freedom. In his autobiography, Parker wrote, "no [night] was too dark or too cold for me to issue forth on a mission of relief and . . . to those who came knocking at my door." Parker kept a log of those he helped but eventually burned it, believing it too dangerous if found. No known pictures of Parker exist, as he feared having his likeness on a wanted poster. A well-read man, Parker believed in education. All eight of his children attended college, many making their living in the education field. As shown in this recent photograph, Parker's home has been restored and is now a museum and national historic site.

This photograph shows the outside of John P. Parker's Phoenix Foundry. Parker was granted several patents for his inventions at the foundry. One was for the Parker Sugar Mill and another for the Parker Pulverizer. Of his days on the Underground Railroad, Parker noted in later life, knowing both the men in Cincinnati and Ripley as he did, that "I can say that Ripley was the real terminus of the Underground Railroad. I worked with both groups after 1845, so I ought to know." Ripley, he said, deserved its reputation as "the hell hole of abolition." Parker's story and the story of Ripley's role in the Underground Railroad is becoming better known. The library of the National Underground Railroad Freedom Center is named the John P. Parker Library, and the freedom center also features a movie dramatization of Parker rescuing slaves. Finally, the Cincinnati Opera has commissioned an opera about Parker from the composer Adolphus Hailstork that is planned for debut in 2007–2008.

John Rankin and John P. Parker were only part of the Underground Railroad in Brown County; the Red Oak Church was considered the next stop after the Rankins' house. This was the parish of the Rev. James Gilliland, who moved from South Carolina in 1805 after members of his congregation complained about his preaching against the "sin of slavery." One of the earliest abolitionists in Brown County, Gilliland would preach and write against slavery for over 35 years.

Although the citizens of Brown County were not all abolitionists, and not all men, many contributed in any way they could to help the runaway slaves. Nancy Collins Armstrong, as a young girl, carried food to the Rankins' home to help feed the fugitives. Her family lived north of the Rankins' home.

At the end of the Sardinia Cemetery, on a small hill, lies the grave of John B. Mahan. Mahan was a minister whose farm was a stop on the Underground Railroad in Brown County. In 1838, Mahan was arrested by the sheriff of Mason County, Kentucky, for a supposed violation of a Kentucky law in Ohio. His crime was helping a Kentucky slave. Mahan was taken to Washington, Kentucky, and held until a trial, some two months later. In that time, his case caused a national uproar. Could an Ohio citizen be tried for helping a Kentucky slave escape, even though the help was rendered in Ohio? The question and the case gained national recognition, and the possible outcome was recognized to have potentially devastating consequences to the abolitionist movement. Mahan was defended by several attorneys, including Chambers Baird of Ripley. Despite perjury on behalf of some prosecution witnesses, the judge at the trial, Walker Reid, who was known for his pro-slavery views, finally ruled that "this court and this jury have no jurisdiction of Mahan's case." While being held in the damp prison, Mahan contracted tuberculosis. Although he died years later in 1844, he was, as his tombstone states, "A Victim to the Slave Powers."

Adam Lowry Rankin, called Lowry, was the Rankins' oldest son. Having no desire to join the ministry and follow in the footsteps of his father, he apprenticed with a carpenter and for a time built steamboats in Ripley. One day in 1834, his life changed. Walking through a steamboat that had docked in Ripley to study its woodwork, he spotted 50 slaves, men and women alike, all chained to a rail and looking "stricken with a hopeless grief." Here Lowry witnessed firsthand one of the slaves being sold to a new owner. Horrified, from then on he pledged to do all he could to end slavery, joining the ministry and becoming a charter member of the Ripley Anti-Slavery Society. In 1862, he became chaplain for the 113th Illinois Regiment and was in several southern military campaigns. In fact, John Rankin had more sons serving as ministers during the Civil War than any other minister in the United States. This rare photograph shows Adam Lowry Rankin with his regiment during the Civil War in Memphis, Tennessee, in either 1863 or 1864, in the center left, where someone has written his name on the photograph.

As the issue of slavery broke out into the Civil War, the county was on the side of the Union, although many citizens could well sympathize with the Southern cause. To prepare, the Ripley Cannon was purchased in Cincinnati at a cost of $1,000. It was a three-inch rifled cannon and was used twice during the war, once near Brooksville, Kentucky, and again on Georgetown Pike to prevent Morgan's Raiders from attacking Ripley.

The Civil War Alarm Bell was used to warn the citizens of Ripley of the approach of the enemy during the Civil War, especially Morgan's Raiders. No record could be found of its use for this purpose. This bell was later moved to the top of the Methodist church tower.

John Hunt Morgan, of Morgan's Raiders fame, was a Confederate general during the Civil War. In July 1863, Morgan was "raiding" through Ohio when he divided his forces into two groups, with one heading toward Georgetown. Once there, Morgan's men, led by his brother, forced the shoe cobbler to fix their shoes while other raiders stole horses and other items. They moved next to Ripley, Red Oak, and Decatur. The other wing of Morgan's men went through Mount Orab and Sardinia, where they burned two bridges.

During the war, when advancing Confederates troops moved toward Cincinnati, Gov. David Tod called for men to defend Ohio's borders. About 1,300 men from Brown County answered the call. The Confederates gave these men the nickname "Squirrel Hunters" because they were said to be "farm boys that never had to shoot at the same squirrel twice." This certificate was for John Beasley of Aberdeen, brother of Massie "Squire" Beasley.

Thousands of men from Brown County fought in the Civil War; in fact, it has been said that someone from Brown County was at every major battle of the war. Men from the county were part of following regiments: the 12th Ohio Volunteers Infantry (OVI), 34th OVI, 47th OVI, 48th OVI, 50th OVI, 59th OVI, 60th OVI, 61st OVI, 70th OVI, and 74th OVI. One soldier who had a unique story to tell was Daniel Boone Reeder of Huntington Township. During the Civil War, he served in the 70th OVI. His injuries occurred at Ezra Church on July 28, 1864, during the battle for Atlanta. Reeder was wounded on the right side of his face, leaving a permanent hole. His solution for repair was to take a spoon and use it to cover the hole, as shown here, creating a local legend in the process.

Ulysses S. Grant was living in Galena, Illinois, when the Civil War started. One of the first Union victories is credited to Grant. At the Battle of Fort Donelson, he gained the nickname "Unconditional Surrender" Grant when he refused to give terms to an old West Point friend. In March 1864, after a series of victories, Pres. Abraham Lincoln sent Grant's nomination in as lieutenant general, giving him three stars, which placed him in command of all the Union armies.

A magnificent horse, this was Cincinnati, Grant's favorite horse. Cincinnati was a superior animal, the son of Lexington, one of the fastest racehorses in history. Grant was given this horse by a St. Louis businessman who happened to have the same last name as Grant. General Grant named the horse and rarely let others ride him, with only two exceptions—childhood friend Adm. Daniel Ammen of Georgetown and President Lincoln.

Maj. Gen. August Kautz was born in Germany and moved with his family to Ripley in 1844. Kautz joined the army during the Mexican-American War and later graduated from West Point. During the Civil War, he was a colonel in the 2nd Ohio Cavalry and chased John Hunt Morgan in both Kentucky and Ohio. Pictured are Kautz (center) and Gen. Phillip Sheridan (right), who were at West Point together.

UNKNOWN
GENERAL PHILLIP SHERIDAN
GENERAL AUGUST VALENTINE KAUTZ
Sepia photograph by Matthew Brady, circa 1864.
(Private collection)

After Pres. Abraham Lincoln was assassinated, Pres. Andrew Johnson ordered the formation of a nine-man military commission, shown here, to try the conspirators being held in connection with the case. The commission included August Kautz of Brown County (third from the left) and Lewis Wallace (who later wrote Ben-Hur). On June 29, 1865, eight people were found guilty. Some were hanged, and some were given life, including Dr. Samuel Mudd. Kautz thought that Mudd was unjustly convicted and worked for many years to clear the doctor's name.

David Ammen shared John Rankin's first house on Front Street in Ripley. Ammen was the editor of the local newspaper, the *Castigator*, which published Rankin's letters on the evils of slavery to his brother Thomas, who had recently purchased a slave. Ammen later printed 1,000 copies of a book based on these letters, entitled *Rankin's Letters on Slavery*, 500 of which were stored in a warehouse in Maysville, Kentucky. During the summer of 1825, the warehouse burned, and arson was determined to be the cause. The remaining copies eventually reached a national audience. Ammen had two sons, Jacob and Daniel, one a general and the other an admiral in the Civil War. Both sons were said to have saved Ulysses S. Grant from disaster. Daniel Ammen was a boyhood friend of Grant's and saved him from drowning in Red Oak Creek. Daniel was later the commander of the Union's Iron Clad Fleet. Jacob Ammen was a Union general who protected Grant's left flank at the Battle of Shiloh and was also a friend of Adam Lowry Rankin. This photograph is of Jacob Ammen in his later years.

The Soldiers and Sailors Monument in Maplewood Cemetery is 40 feet tall and made of Barre granite. The monument was unveiled on Decoration Day in 1885, in a ceremony attended by former president Rutherford B. Hayes and Ohio governor Charles Grosvenor. Some 12,000 to 15,000 people were believed to have attended. The monument and ceremony were the work of the Civil War veterans' association in Ripley, the Grand Army of the Republic, usually called the GAR.

The Liberty Monument in Ripley was dedicated in 1912. It has four bronze plaques that honor Ripley's heroes. One plaque lists abolitionists from Brown County, another lists forerunners of the abolitionists, the third lists the generals and admirals from the area, and the last lists the companies of infantry, cavalry, and navy from Ripley. This photograph of a gathering before the monument is interesting, not only for its historical value but because it is not known what the occasion was.

Four years after the war's end Ulysses S. Grant was elected the 18th president of the United States. His military career had been outstanding, but his presidency was not. Grant returned to Georgetown several times; his last visit was in 1880 when he was stumping for James Garfield. Interestingly, in both the 1868 and 1872 elections, Grant did not carry his home county. Brown County was a solid Democratic county and voted against its native son.

Here the First Presbyterian Church in Ripley is decorated for the memorial service for Grant not long after his death. The service was held on August 8, 1885, at 2:00 p.m. Members of the local GAR met at their hall and marched to the church to honor their former neighbor and late commander.

The Rankin land has changed over the years. This picture shows the many trees, fences, and outbuildings that are now no longer on the property. This photograph is undated, although it is probably from the early 20th century. The children pictured are unknown.

Pictured here are three of the Rankins' 13 children. From left to right are Thomas Lovejoy (or T. L.), John T. Jr., and Rev. Arthur Tappan. Arthur Tappan was the Rankins' eighth son and was 51 years old when his father died. Both John T. Jr. and Thomas Lovejoy assisted escaping slaves. Thomas Lovejoy once escorted runaway slaves all the way to Canada.

John Rankin died at the age of 93 in 1886, in Ironton, Ohio. Six years after his death, many of his family, friends, and former neighbors gathered to honor him with a bust on his tombstone. Rankin's surviving sons are the four bearded men on the right, in the front row. The African American woman second from the right of the tombstone came to Rankin's house as a baby and was left at the Rankins' by her escaping slave mother, who later came back to Ripley to raise her. At the same time this photograph was taken, Jim Crow laws were in effect south of the Ohio River. In his autobiography, written in his 80th year, Rankin wrote of the blessing that none of his children or grandchildren were killed in the Civil War, but he was pained that the war had occurred at all. "I lived to see four million slaves liberated, but not in the way I had long labored it be done."

In 1890, the GAR, veterans of the Civil War, gathered from all over Brown County to meet in Higginsport. Capt. Frederick Kautz, a leading citizen, is on the far left. In the background are David Boles' Blacksmith shop and the Harry Troutman's Saloon.

SOLDIERS' MONUMENT, DECATUR, OHIO.
ERECTED BY
The Manchester Granite & Marble Co., Manchester, Ohio

The Soldiers' Monument in Decatur sits in the center of the Decatur Park, which was dedicated in 1908. It was made of Barre granite by the Manchester Granite and Marble Company of Manchester, Ohio, and was 19.5 feet tall. It was dedicated to all the soldiers who went to war from Byrd Township. The statue fell in 1976 and was repaired and replaced in 1987.

Three

TOBACCO

The importance of tobacco is made clear from the Brown County flag, which prominently shows a tobacco leaf. In 1953, the Brown County Historical Society held a contest for the design of the flag in which school students submitted designs. An art class at Wilmington College was the final judge, and it had to pick from 75 entries. The winners were Jerry McKenzie and Kenneth Brookbank, both fourth graders at Higginsport School. The field of the flag is brown, both for the fertile soil and for the name of the county; the circle is yellow for the O in Ohio; and the 16 stars are for the 16 townships. In the center, most prominent, is a tobacco plant. Because of the tobacco plant pictured, an antismoking group recently complained about this flag, flying at the statehouse in Columbus alongside the other 87 flags from the counties in Ohio.

This is the front and back of a card that was given out by the Independent Warehouse in Ripley. It lists the average price for tobacco per pound from 1923 until 1928. A pound of tobacco in 1928 was almost the same as the price of a carton of cigarettes is today.

A tobacco bed, like the one shown here, is used to start a tobacco plant, which is then replanted. The bed cover is spread to hold the heat of the early spring sunlight and to protect the plants from frost. One of the hardest jobs in raising tobacco was the pulling of the plants out of the bed. In this picture, Cecil Scaggs shows Ernie Stivers his tobacco bed.

When planting tobacco, the young plants are placed in the "fingers" of the carousel on the planting machine, shown here. As it rotates, the machine plants the seedling in the ground. The tobacco patch will sometimes need to be hoed and watered, depending on the season. Once the tobacco plants are growing well, they will begin to produce shoots from the joint of each leaf with the stalk. These "suckers" divert growth from the leaves. They are removed in a process known as "suckering," which is usually done by hand several times during the season. Later the plant will produce a flower cluster at its top. In order to make the leaves grow larger, the plant is "topped" by cutting off these flowers. Tobacco is a very unique plant; the seed is one of smallest, about the size of a mustard seed, and it is not uncommon for a plant to grow close to six feet.

55

Once mature, the tobacco plant is harvested, cut, and put on sticks, then hung in a barn to dry. It then must be removed from the stalk and put in "hands" and pressed in preparation for sale. These men are checking to see if the tobacco is "in case," or damp enough to be taken from the stalk without crumbling. Curing methods vary with the type of tobacco grown, and tobacco barn design varies accordingly. Air-cured tobacco is hung in well-ventilated barns and allowed to dry over a period of weeks. Fire-cured tobacco is hung in large barns where smoldering fires of hardwoods are kept burning. The aging process then continues for a period of months. Tobacco does have other uses; "tobacco water" is a traditional organic insecticide that can be used in gardening by boiling tobacco in water. When cool, the mixture can be applied with a spray or painted onto the leaves of garden plants, where it will prove deadly to insects.

This interesting photograph shows a John Parker Tobacco Press inside Parker's Phoenix Foundry. The dried tobacco is removed from the stalk in a process called "stripping" the tobacco. The tobacco would then be put in "hands" and then pressed into a hogshead barrel using the Parker press. White burley tobacco, today the most commonly grown tobacco in the world, was first grown in 1864 in Brown County by George Webb, on the farm of Capt. Frederick Kautz. Webb planted red burley he had purchased and found that a few of the seedlings had a whitish look. "He transplanted them to the fields anyway, where they grew into mature plants but retained their light color. The cured leaves had an exceedingly fine texture and were exhibited as a curiosity at the market in Cincinnati. The following year he planted ten acres from seeds from those plants, which brought a premium at auction. *White Burley*, as it was later called, became the main component in chewing tobacco, American blend pipe tobacco, and American-style cigarettes."

The first tobacco warehouse in Ripley was the Union Loose Leaf Warehouse, which opened around 1912. For many years, the singsong voice of the auctioneer would end with the drawn-out name of the buyer: S-o-o-l-d to American, or Liggett-Myers, or Reynolds. This was money in the bank for Brown County tobacco farmers.

The old Ohio-Kentucky, or O-K, Warehouse in Ripley was destroyed by a tornado a few years ago and was replaced by the new O-K Warehouse. In the past, the tobacco was auctioned off in the warehouses from Monday through Friday, early December through February.

58

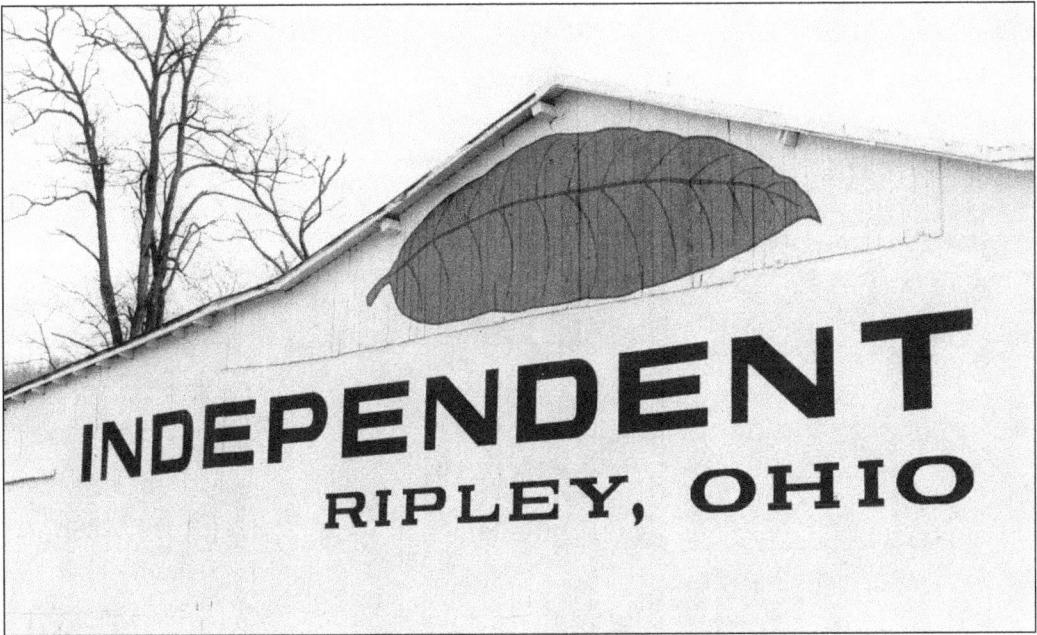

The Independent Warehouse had a tough history. Since it was located on Front Street in Ripley, this warehouse was often caught in the various floods through the years. Finally the warehouse was destroyed by a fire in 2001. Currently there are plans to turn the lot where this warehouse once stood into a park.

Inside the Independent Warehouse in 1926, this photograph shows some of the workers and officers of the warehouse. Some of the people in the photograph are Harv Drake, John F. Paeltz, Ralph Paeltz, Joseph Klinker, Martin Klinker, and Clarence Klinker.

In 1913, the Loose Leaf Warehouse of Georgetown was located near the entrance to the Brown County Fairgrounds. Some of the people pictured here among the tobacco are Robert Cochran, Sam Kutz, "Mit" Bohner, "Shorty" Harris, Frank Ellsberry, "Ol" Wilhaus, Hite Tyler, and John Kestler. When the market opened in 1913, 12,000 people were present for the first sale, in which 150,000 pounds were sold in one day.

This tobacco leaf is actually a sewing kit provided as an incentive by the Farmers Warehouse for farmers to bring their tobacco to its warehouse for the highest prices. The tobacco auctions brought a lot of business to Brown County. For several weeks, the auctioneers would stay at local motels and hotels, and the farmers would also come into town to watch their tobacco sell and then have dinner, and maybe celebrate the profit they made.

Sometimes getting the tobacco to the warehouses or other markets required some ingenuity. In the winter of 1917, the Ohio River froze, and ferries could not run. This gentleman had to use horses and sleds to get his tobacco to market in Kentucky. Maysville, Kentucky, had more markets than Ripley, but farmers often took their crop from Ohio to Kentucky or vice versa.

In this photograph, Cora and Frank Wiley are shown in front of their house in Ripley in 1919. Today this house is the Ohio Tobacco Museum, which is dedicated to saving the history of this controversial plant so important to the economy of Brown County.

The 1964 dedication of a marker commemorating the first planting of white burley tobacco in Higginsport is shown here, attended by then governor Jim Rhodes and James Frederick Robinson, whose grandfather had first grown the plant. For many years, this marker was on an experimental farm in Red Oak run by the Ohio State University. With the closing of that facility, it was moved to the Ohio Tobacco Museum in Ripley. Today tobacco is a controversial plant. Many farms do not grow it anymore, some planting soybeans or corn instead. In 2004, a buyout program was passed into law, allowing $9.6 billion to be paid to growers and quota owners over 10 years. Tobacco product manufacturers and importers fund the buyout based on their share of the U.S. tobacco products market. The bill ended the federal program regulating tobacco production and sales.

Four

THE OHIO RIVER

This 1915 view shows the Ohio River and Ripley. The role of the river in the lives of Brown County citizens cannot be overstated—it was the original interstate highway—the economy, leisure activities, and tourism all depended on it. But sometimes, in the case of floods, the river could be devastating. The name "Ohio" comes from a Native American word meaning "beautiful river," and few would disagree with that statement. Historically the Ohio River was very shallow in summer and choked with ice in the winter, making river travel, both for pleasure and commerce, difficult. In this interesting photograph, one can clearly see the Piano Factory building just to the right of center. To the right and slightly forward of that is the Phoenix Foundry area. The old Union School can be seen in the center of the photograph. Note the planted hillside, which is covered with trees today.

This is a 1908 bird's-eye view of Aberdeen with Maysville, Kentucky, on the bottom. Aberdeen was named after Aberdeen, Scotland. Nathan Ellis started a ferry between Fishing Gut Creek and Limestone (Maysville) in 1796. He built the first home in Aberdeen, and Evan Campbell built a hotel there not long after that.

As seen in this photograph from 1921, travel by river was very busy because the bridge to Maysville was not built until the early 1930s. This photograph was taken from the Kentucky side, which is where the train station was located.

The Boudes, or Augusta, Ferry is located west of Higginsport. The original ferry was started by John Boude. Born in Pennsylvania, he later moved to Maysville, Kentucky, where he bought 400 acres on the Ohio side of the Ohio River and started a ferry. Here is a picture of the ferry from the 1960s.

There have been various owners of the ferry through the years, and today it is the only ferry still in operation between Cincinnati and Maysville. The ferryboat *Dr. George Mackey* was one of the boats that operated at Boudes Ferry. The *Dr. George Mackey* was built in Cincinnati in 1874.

The *Argand* was built in Levanna in 1896 and named after an oil refinery below Marietta, Ohio. A sternwheel packet boat, it worked the Wheeling-Parkersburg trade for a number of years, until it was sold to the Big Sandy Navigation Company, which used it on that river. Although it caught fire and sank, perhaps the most interesting story surrounding the *Argand* was one of its captains. Around 1897, one of the *Argand's* original owners, Capt. Gordon Greene of the Greene Line Steamers, Inc., bought out his original partner, Capt. Newt Flescher. Unable to pay another captain, his wife, Mary, became captain of the *Argand*. She was the only licensed woman steamboat pilot and captain on the Ohio and Mississippi Rivers and guided steamboats between Cincinnati and Charleston, West Virginia, for many years. In 1947, one of Greene's sons bought the famous *Delta Queen*, and Mary moved aboard. In 1949, after 59 years of steamboating and making her home on one of the 28 steamers owned by their company, Mary passed away quietly one night on the *Delta Queen*.

The Ripley Wharf boat was used for steamboat landings, as a permanent wharf moored to the land was impractical because of continual changes in the level of the river. Steamboats moored alongside the wharf boat to disembark passengers and freight.

This photograph shows two riverboats tied to the Ripley Wharf, the *Chilo* and the *Greenland*. The *Greenland* was another boat owned by the Greene Line Steamers, Inc. It had 54 cabins and staterooms and made four trips from the Ohio River to the world's fair in St. Louis in 1904. Mary Greene, famous riverboat captain, gave birth aboard the *Greenland* to her son Tom, who would later become an owner of the *Delta Queen*.

No, that is not Tom Sawyer looking at his riverboat, but it looks like it could be an Ohio version of that famous character. The *E. A. Woodruff*, shown here, was a snag boat that worked the Ohio River removing debris and other items from the river. When this photograph was taken, it was working just down river from Ripley. First deployed in 1929, the snag boats, or "Uncle Sam's tooth pullers" as they came to be known, "ran full steam into the snags, jarring them loose. The limbs were then hoisted and broken apart on the vessel's deck. They were unlike anything known elsewhere in the world, and their impact was dramatic. Insurance and shipping rates dropped, and the number of steamboats on the Mississippi and Ohio Rivers increased significantly." The *E. A. Woodruff* was eventually retired and became a wharf boat in Louisville.

The Maddox Drug Company produced many postcards of Brown County. This card is of the riverboat *Courier* pulling away from the Ripley Wharf boat to head up river. In 1895, this riverboat started the Cincinnati-to-Maysville trade that it ran for 22 years. It was at first owned by the White Collar Line, and in 1904, Capt. Gordon Greene purchased it for the Greene line. It was dismantled at Ashland, Kentucky, in 1918.

Pictured here is the *Wonderland*, one of the last of the showboats. These types of boats often stopped in towns along the Ohio River, providing entertainment to the area. Clarence Dragoo of Ripley worked for many years in the band on this boat. He told the story of the boat docking once in Paducah, Kentucky, when typhoid broke out. The entire ship was quarantined for two weeks before they could leave the dock.

Here is the showboat *Goldenrod* docked in Ripley. Built in 1909, it was considered the largest and finest showboat ever built, being 200 feet long and 45 feet wide, with over 2,500 electric lights and seating for more than 1,400 people. It has been moved several times, and now the City of St. Charles, Missouri, owns it. It is now a national historical landmark.

Ice was often a hazard for boats, big and small, along the river. This is the *Greenwood* as it sits in the frozen Ohio River near Ripley. This sternwheeler was built in 1898 and was one of the main boats for the Greene Line Steamers, Inc., of Cincinnati. It often ran from Cincinnati to Charleston with many stops along the way, including Brown County. It sank in 1925 just above the suspension bridge in Cincinnati when the *Chris Greene* backed into it.

The Aberdeen boat landing was a busy place during the winter of 1917–1918. On the left is the *Laurance*, which was built in 1891 in Madison, Indiana. It was the ferry between Maysville and Aberdeen at the time. In 1930, it burned at Maysville but was rebuilt and ran until the Simon Kenton Memorial Bridge was built. Even then it was not done and was sold to Manchester, Ohio, and renamed the *Col. W. S. Taylor.*

Ripley and Levanna had very active shipyards building riverboats. Pictured here is the riverboat *Slack Barret*, which was the last boat built in the Levanna boatyard. It was built in 1916 or 1917.

The Simon Kenton Memorial Bridge is a suspension bridge built in 1931 and originally opened with a toll, which was removed in 1945. Its main span is 1,060 feet long, and the total length of the bridge is 1,991 feet. The ferryboat *Kiwana*, shown below the bridge, ran from Aberdeen to Maysville for many years.

The Simon Kenton Memorial Bridge was recently given a makeover. It was originally painted silver, then for many years was green, and is now silver again. In 2000, a new bridge was built just a few miles west of this bridge, named after Ohio congressman William Harsha. It connects West Aberdeen to the AA Highway in Kentucky.

Floods are a way of life for towns along the Ohio River, and Brown County is no exception. This photograph is of the flood of 1884, the biggest flood of the century and one of the four largest ever recorded on the Ohio. The flood stage in Cincinnati was recorded at 71.1 feet.

In this photograph, the Second Street Bridge in Ripley is covered from the 1907 flood, which cut off Ripley from Hestoria. The Ohio River hit twice that year with floods; the first crested on January 21 at 65.2 feet, and the second flood crested on March 19 at 62.1 feet.

This is from the 1913 flood in Ripley at the corner of Main and Front Streets looking west down Front Street. The flood has put both the wharf boat and ferryboat almost on top of the street. On the right are the top of the Union School and the spire of the Methodist church.

This view looks west on Second Street in Ripley during the 1913 flood. The Methodist church and Union School are in the distance. To the left is the Maddox Drug Company, and to the right of it on the opposite corner is the Ripley National Bank. The trees at the extreme left are where the Union Township Public Library now stands.

Two of Ripley's former movie theaters, the Wigwam and the New York, are shown during a 1913 flood. It is not sure which flood this was in 1913 because there were two floods that year. A flood in January crested at 62.2 feet on the 14th, and the second flood reached a level of 69.9 feet when it crested on April 1.

It is not known if this photograph was taken during the January or April flood of 1913, but it must have been taken either on the Liberty Steps or near Liberty Hill and the Rankin House. Red Oak Creek is very high, and it looks like the water is over the Second Street Bridge. The spire of St. Michaels Church is in the foreground.

Apparently a flood will not keep the more stylish citizens from getting to their destinations. This 1913 photograph shows Main Street near Easton Street where the trains went through Ripley. Notice that the flood has almost covered the first floor of the businesses along Main Street. On the right, the Railroad Crossing sign is almost covered.

Before the Ohio River was deepened, it was not unusual for it to freeze. Riverboats could not pass, but citizens could sometimes walk across it. This person is walking toward Ripley during the winter of 1917–1918. Front Street and the end of Main Street are in the center of the photograph.

This remarkable photograph was taken during the January 1937 flood, showing a house on Cherry Street in Ripley. The 1937 flood was among the most devastating to hit the Ohio River. From Pittsburgh, Pennsylvania, to Cairo, Illinois, 385 people were killed, 1 million were left homeless, and property losses eclipsed the $500 million mark. If one looks carefully at the photograph, it is possible to see that most of the windows are still intact.

Devastation left by the 1937 flood is shown in this view, which looks north on Main Street in Ripley. It is likely that those are rolls of wallpaper that were damaged by the flood and were put on the curb to wait for disposal.

More damage from 1937 can be seen this photograph. Front Street in Ripley looks more like a mud-covered path after the 1937 flood receded. The house on the left was the Russell family home and later the home of Dr. George Tyler. Many of the trees on both sides of the street are gone today.

The power of water is shown here in this photograph taken from Second Street in Ripley looking at Cherry Street. If one looks carefully, it is possible to see that a building is completely upside down. The 1937 flood was the highest flood in recorded history of the Ohio River, reaching 80 feet.

Harold Paeltz took this 1945 photograph of his family. The Ohio River crested on March 7 at 69.2 feet, making it the fourth-deepest flood in Ripley history. The rowboat is on the steps of the Union Township Public Library at the corner of Main and Second Streets, with Bristow's Drug Store in the background.

This photograph is undated but may have been taken in 1945. The car is from the 1930s, but the clothes on the people seem a little later. The car is at Main and Second Streets, and Bristow's Drug Store is in the background. It looks like this car could be flooded. That could be AAA in the rowboat, coming to bail them out.

From April 17, 1948, a flood gauge on the Second Street Bridge over Red Oak Creek in Ripley appears to indicate the flood was up to almost 64 feet. The official record says that the river crested the next day at 64.8 feet. So the flood rose another eight inches in a 24-hour period.

This photograph is from the U.S. Army Corps of Engineers in Huntington, West Virginia, and shows the Ohio River flood of March 12, 1964, at Aberdeen. Notice that in the lower left of this photograph, U.S. 52 is closed due to the flood, but the Simon Kenton Memorial Bridge is open, and many people have crossed the river to see the damage.

Five

BUSINESS AND INDUSTRY

The Ohio River and Columbus Railway was known by two other names, the ORC and the "Old Rough and Crooked." Its office and depot was in Ripley at Easton Alley. The line was started in 1903 with the plan to connect Maysville, Kentucky, with Columbus, Ohio, but this plan never materialized, and in 1916, the line was sold in a sheriff's sale.

Another railroad with a great nickname, the Cincinnati, Georgetown, and Portsmouth Railroad was also known to locals as the "Come, Go, & Push." It operated from Cincinnati through Georgetown into Russellville from 1904 until 1934. The line was never completed to Portsmouth. This is the traction bridge near Russellville and is 85 feet off the ground.

The foundry business had a long history in Ripley. The Phoenix Foundry was started by John P. Parker and later sold to the Russell family, who operated it for many years. This photograph is from inside the Ripley Foundry and Machine Company of Harry L. Russell, shown on the right, who was one of the brothers who owned and operated the business.

Bristow's Drug Store is a major landmark for many in Ripley. People stopped at the drugstore for a drink from the soda fountain and to catch up on the latest news. In the late 1920s and early 1930s, Bristow's Pharmacy had a monthly newsletter called the *Bristow's Broadcaster*, which was mailed to customers' homes. Each issue was eight pages and had articles on general health with advertisements for products in the store.

From 1869 until 1885, the Ohio Valley Piano Company operated in Ripley. By 1876, the company had produced over 1,800 pianos of various types with plans to build 500 more that year. The company produced grand, square, and upright pianos, with the Valley Gem and Grande Scale being their most popular models. Today the Ripley Museum has a Valley Gem from 1870. In 1890, Baldwin took over manufacturing of the Valley Gem brand.

The Ripley National Bank was founded in 1862, and in 1864, it became one of the earliest chartered banks. It was always located at Main and Second Streets and used the slogan "Ripley's Bank of Service." This picture is from the 1920s and shows, from left to right, Evelyn Hayes, C. D. Norris, Mary Norris, Lulu Buchanan, Thomas Goldsberry, and Earl Hayes.

The Citizens Bank of Higginsport was organized in 1901 and moved to the current location at the corner of Washington and Jackson Streets in 1913, before this photograph was taken in 1917. The business has grown for many years under the leadership of Dwight Marriott and now has two branches outside of Higginsport.

Today it is common to hear the phrase one-stop shopping. This photograph proves it is not a new concept. This is Shelton's Grocery and Bank in Aberdeen. Pictured are Aultman (left) and Delosse Shelton and their parents, C. B. and Minnie Shelton. According to local lore, a bank in Aberdeen accepted Confederate money at the start of the Civil War. Perhaps it was this one?

Brown County had many small stores such as John Campbell's, located at the intersection of Scofield Road and Martin Hill Road. This picture is from the early 1900s. The man holding the broom is Dudley Bloomfield, and he is standing in front Campbell's Huckster Wagon.

The Decatur Supply House was owned and operated by E. M. Rickey, and this photograph was probably taken in the late 1920s or early 1930s. It sold Red Top Flour, Sohio Gasoline, and Tuxedo Seeds, which are just a few of the items advertised at the store.

This is a wonderful photograph showing the Ripley Hardware Company decorated for Ripley's centennial in 1912. Pictured are Albert (left) and Charlie Liggett. Today this building is the director's room of the Oak Hills Bank.

George Frank's meat shop in Ripley is shown here, and yes, those are skinned rabbits hanging on the left. Frank was such a successful businessman that he was made a director of the Citizens National Bank, later becoming its vice president. Frank, shown here at left, was also a politician, having been elected Brown County commissioner. He died in 1932.

The interior of Smith's Grocery in Ripley is shown in this photograph owned by a Brown County resident. Many will recall this store by the name West End Grocery when Louis Klinker owned it. The photograph is from 1955, and pictured here are, from left to right, Bob Carpenter, unidentified, Rick Klinker, Mildred Klein Klinker (Rick's mother), and Vern Smith. At least skinned animals are not hanging from the building.

Today, while driving on U.S. 62, a person might pass through Ash Ridge, which has only a dozen or so houses. But some may remember a store in Ash Ridge. It was the E. F. Hancock Grocery store and also served as the local post office. From the advertisements in the windows, it appears toilet supplies and turpentine were sold at very nice prices.

Almost every small town in Brown County had a general store for the wants and needs of the community. This old photograph is of the Garrison Grocery store in Russellville around the beginning of the 20th century. Owners Katy and Clarence Garrison are shown in the center.

The back of this old photograph is labeled as the Cincinnati, Georgetown, and Portsmouth Railroad (CG&P) crew working on the fill on Day Hill Road to open the line to Russellville. The date of the photograph is unknown, and the individuals are unidentified.

Mechanized farming came early to Brown County, as seen in this photograph. An early tractor is shown, with some field hands getting ready for the day's work. This type of early machinery is showcased each year in the Ohio Valley Antique Machinery Show, which, as of 2006, is in its 36th year.

The Sullivan Shoe Factory in Georgetown was built in 1931. William J. Sullivan employed 50 workers on opening, but as his business grew, he increased his workforce, reaching a peak of 415 women making 3,100 shoes a day. Most of these jobs were lost in 1967 when the shoe factory, shown in this photograph, burned.

As part of employment at the shoe factory, a class was held in which students learned to work in a shoe factory. The class of 1937 is shown in this photograph. They received diplomas from the State of Ohio that were signed by the superintendent of the Georgetown Board of Education.

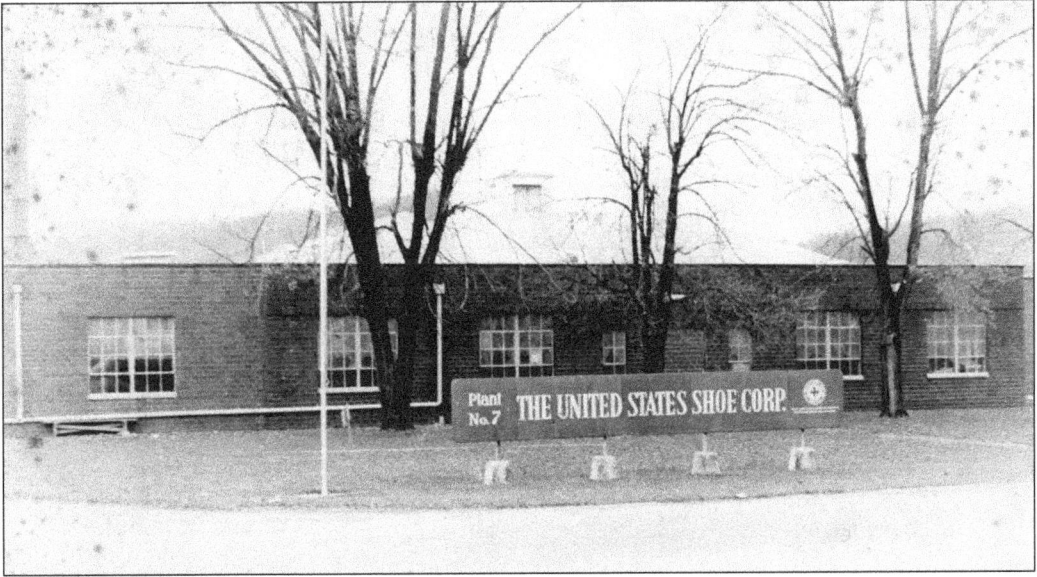

The Ripley United States Shoe Corporation plant started on Second Street in 1952 and at one time was the largest employer in Brown County with 450 employees. In its first year of operation, the factory made 200 pairs of shoes a day, but later production was increased with new manufacturing methods to a peak of 6,000 pairs of shoes a day. The factory closed on December 17, 1992, a few weeks after its 40th anniversary.

The Georgetown Grist Mill is located on Route 221 a mile outside of the village. This mill was built in 1843 by Edward Thompson and was also known as "Tunnel Mill" since the millrace tunneled through a nearby hill. In 1883, it became the Schuster Mill. A gristmill was used to grind grains such as wheat, rye, oats, and barely into flour or meal.

Pavement comes to Georgetown. This photograph shows one of the first street pavings in the village on the corner of Cherry and Main Streets. The buildings on the right on Main Street were destroyed by a fire in 2001. It is interesting to note the equipment and methods used at this time.

Across from the Brown County Courthouse Square was a fine example of a local business. Markley and Jacobs sold "staple and fancy groceries" in the late 1800s and early 1900s. In many ways, this photograph shows the migration and growth of Brown County. With the damages from floods and the use of trains and later cars, the population of Brown County moved away from the river to towns like Georgetown and Mount Orab.

The Pohl Garage in Georgetown was at the corner State and Apple Streets. It is believed to be the first garage for working on automobiles in Brown County and one of the first in Ohio. Someone that knows about antique cars might be able to identify the year, make, and model of the two cars in the picture.

Many will recall the Lake Grant Motel, especially its neon sign of Gen. Ulysses S. Grant, which shined out front. It was on U. S. 68 in Mount Orab and was owned and operated by R. E. Lukemire and his wife. Their motto was that "it makes a whale of a difference whose bed you sleep in."

Few readers will recall the Third Street Bridge in Ripley that went over Red Oak Creek and connected Ripley with Hestoria. The iron bridge was moved to Ripley in 1883 or 1885, depending on which source one reads, from Aberdeen. The bridge was rebuilt in 1922. The bridge connected Third Street to what is now Circle Drive.

Brown County has had many covered bridges; one of them was the Scofield Covered Bridge, also known as Martin's Hill Bridge. It spanned the east fork of Eagle Creek, or Beetle Creek, about four miles outside of Ripley on Scofield Road. The bridge was built in 1875 by local contractor John Griffith and replaced in 1989.

Six

ARTS AND LEISURE

Frank Gregg was born in Ripley and later moved to Cleveland, where he worked as a newspaper writer. He was important to helping Ripley's role in the Underground Railroad become more widely known, as he helped to write the autobiography of John P. Parker, *His Promised Land*. For the 1912 Ripley centennial, Gregg paid for the Front Street Monument and tablets for various historic homes around the town.

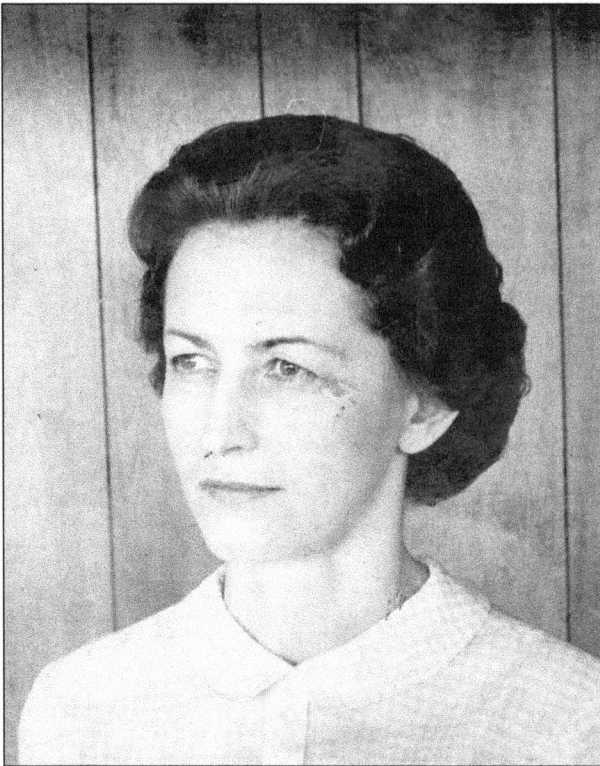

Miriam Stivers Zachman was the daughter of A. J. Stivers and Eliese Bambach Stivers. Zachman worked hard to preserve the history of Brown County, helping to compile and write *Ripley, Ohio—Its History and Families* in the early 1960s. Zachman and her sister donated their mother's home to house the Ripley Museum and gave financial support to many organizations in the county.

Jess Bier was a local historian and businessman who organized the Old Timers Building at the Brown County Fairgrounds. Bier wrote a column for many years in the *News Democrat* about the history of Brown County. He died in 1964. Because of his work and the work of others, much of Brown County's history was saved for future generations.

Another Brown County historian was Carl Thompson. Thompson was the author of *Historical Collections of Brown County,* published in 1969. This 1,340-page work represented a lifetime of research for Thompson, who was born in Levanna. He also published *Treasures of Pisgah and Levanna, Ohio* three years before his Brown County history.

The old Brown County Jail building, built in 1870 and used until the latter half of the 20th century as a jail, it is now the home of the Brown County Historical Society and the Brown County Genealogical Society. Eloise Dickerson was the president of the Brown County Historical Society at the time the building was acquired for the society, and through her generosity, she ensured that the history of Brown County had a home.

Musician Joe "Fox" Smith was born in Ripley in 1902 to a family with six brothers, all of whom were musicians. One day, Smith packed his cornet in a paper sack and left Ohio for New York. He found success playing trumpet and cornet with Fletcher Henderson and Ethel Waters and was famous as Bessie Smith's favorite accompanist. Smith was noted by the legendary John Hammond to be "one of the most amazing musicians the world has ever known." In 1924, Smith was trumpeter with the Fletcher Henderson Orchestra, the top African American band at the time. To accept a better-paying job with a Broadway pit orchestra, he left the band suddenly, leaving Henderson to scramble for a replacement who might be as good as Smith had been. Henderson heard of someone who might work out from Chicago and hired him. That someone was Louis Armstrong, and the rest, as they say, is history. Smith died at the age of 36, although one can still hear his artistry on many recordings still available today.

Cora Young Wiles was born in Ripley in 1864. Her father, W. D. Young, a former Civil War veteran, had been mayor of Ripley for 10 years. Wiles graduated from the Cincinnati College of Music and was a talented musician. She wrote "The Ripley Song" for the 1912 centennial of Ripley. She was listed in the 1914 edition of *Woman's Who's Who of America*, where her many activities were noted. Her entry also indicated that she favored women's suffrage.

Jens Jensen was an artist who emigrated from Denmark and worked at the famous Rookwood Pottery in Cincinnati from 1928 to 1948. When the Rookwood Pottery closed, Jensen and his wife moved to Brown County and opened Gamtofte Pottery. Although it eventually closed, today Jensen is one of the more famous Rookwood artists. His work sells for up to several thousand dollars, and his paintings are also becoming more popular.

Rosa Washington Riles, better known as "Aunt Jemima," was born in 1901 in Red Oak. Riles became Aunt Jemima in the 1950s while employed as a cook in the home of a Quaker Oats executive. Riles was sent out on pancake demonstrations, and because of her charisma and personality, she became a customer favorite. Riles died in 1969 and is buried in the Presbyterian Cemetery at Red Oak.

For many in Brown County, the place to be on a Saturday night was the Roselawn. Dinner and dancing were provided by owner George Keramis and his band, the Kentucky Kavaliers, shown here in this picture from the 1950s. It was located on Second Street between the Union Loose Leaf Warehouse and the O-K Warehouse. Behind the building were several tourist cabins and dozens of rosebushes, from which the Roselawn got its name.

Harry "Slim" Sallee was a left-handed crossfire pitcher who possessed outstanding control. Born in Higginsport, Sallee was discovered while playing ball in southern Ohio. He holds two records: fewest pitched balls in a nine-inning game, with 65, and more wins than walks with 20 in 1919. He spent his first eight years in professional baseball with the St. Louis Cardinals and then played for the New York Giants, finally returning home to Ohio in 1919 to lead the Cincinnati Reds, with his 21 wins, to a world championship. Many may know this championship year as the year of the infamous Black Sox World Series in which eight White Sox players, including Chicago star outfielder "Shoeless" Joe Jackson, conspired to throw games. The Reds players insisted they would have won anyway, but history remembers only the scandal.

Amateur baseball was often front-page news in the local newspapers. The 1923 Ripley baseball team, pictured here, played in the Blue Grass League, which included teams from both sides of the Ohio River. The championship game that year was between two Brown County teams, Ripley and Georgetown, and was called the "Little World Series." The series games were played at the Brown County Fairgrounds, with Ripley winning the championship.

Albert Nelson Marquis was born in Decatur in 1855 and grew up in Hamersville. He started his own publishing company in Cincinnati and moved it to Chicago in 1884. At first, he specialized in business directories, but in 1899, he tried something new, publishing the first edition of *Who's Who in America*. It was an immediate success and has inspired many similar references books. Marquis's book, which is a listing of biographical information about important living Americans, is still found in libraries today.

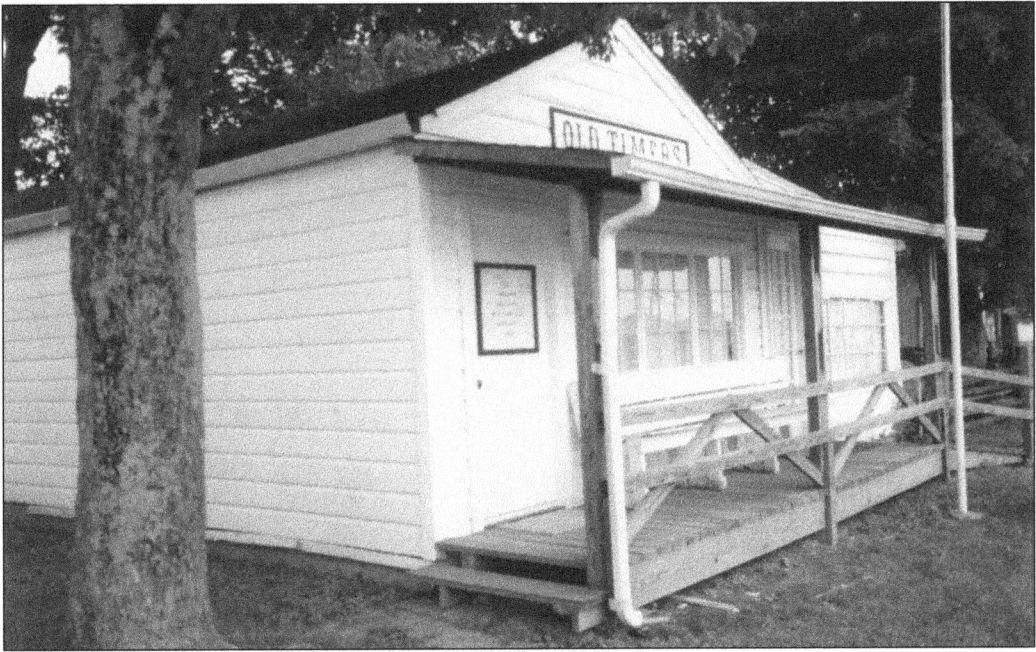

Originally begun in a tent in the 1950s with photographs pinned to the wall, today the Old Timers Building is at the Brown County Fairgrounds. Now run by the Brown County Historical Society, the interior features many photographs from Brown County's history for fair visitors to view.

This aerial view shows the Brown County Fairgrounds in Georgetown, sometime in the 1960s. The Brown County Fair is called the "Little State Fair" and is one of the biggest and oldest fairs in Ohio. The first fair was held in 1850 in Russellville, and two years later, it moved to the current fairgrounds, where it has been ever since. Attendance today makes it the third most visited fair in Ohio; 2006 celebrated the 154th annual fair.

Truly Blue was a beloved horse in Brown County. He was owned by Charles Troute of Russellville and participated in many horse shows, winning at the Brown County Fair from 1909 until 1925. He died in the fairgrounds ring in 1925 when he caught his leg in the harness of a competitor. He was buried at the fairgrounds.

The Brown County Fair was not the only fair in the county; many of the villages had their own fairs. The Yellow Ribbon Fair was the annual fair at Aberdeen. This photograph is from the first fair in October 1893, and the last fair was in 1914. The grounds were on State Route 41 across from Fishing Gut Creek.

104

This Ripley Fair was held at the Ripley Fairgrounds, which is where the Ripley Union Huntington Lewis Elementary School is today. The grounds comprised 12 acres, with floral and mechanical halls and over 100 stalls for pigs and horses. Fairs were held almost every year from 1855 to 1929, when the Great Depression ended the fair. Advertising for the fair could be simple, as this photograph shows. That is Clarence Klinker driving and Eugene Drake his passenger.

Star Lake in Mount Orab was a beautiful Sunday getaway for many in Adams, Brown, and Clermont Counties, as this postcard from 1941 shows. The lake is gone now. When Route 32 was built, the extra dirt was used to fill in the lake.

The 17 men and women in this photograph made up the Sardinia Band. Many of the local towns had a band much like this one that often gave concerts in the warmer months for the entertainment of the village. Interestingly, the ladies in the band have rather official-looking hats on, while the men do not.

The Aberdeen Frisch's Big Boy was a popular spot for many people. Weekend nights often found teenagers from both sides of the river "cruising" Frisch's parking lot. Many enjoyed the curb service of a Big Boy and onion rings with a cold Coke. Frisch's is now gone, but for many, the memories still last.

Seven

PEOPLE AND PLACES

One of the more inspiring people researched for this book, Charles Young was born near Mayslick, Kentucky, the son of former slaves. He graduated with honors from the all-white high school at Ripley in 1880 at the age of 16, won appointment to the United States Military Academy at West Point in 1884, and in 1889 became the third African American to graduate from the school. Young went on to teach military science at Wilberforce University as well as serving in Mexico, the Philippines, Haiti, Liberia, and Mexico while in the army. He was also superintendent of Sequoia and General Grant National Parks and was an accomplished musician and composer. It was said that "he played a very important role in giving all Americans awareness that a Black man could be an outstanding soldier, teacher, diplomat, and patriot." At the outset of World War I, Young was the highest-ranking African American in the army.

THE LATE
**Col.
Charles
Young**

RESCUED TEDDY
ROOSEVELT AND
HIS FAMOUS
"ROUGH RIDERS"
AT SAN JUAN
HILL.

WEST POINT GRADUATE.
MILITARY ATTACHÉ
HAITI, LIBERIA.

SPINGARN MEDAL
1915

LIEUT.
CLARENCE
DAVENPORT

LIEUT.
ROBERT
TRESVILLE

IN THE
PHILIPPINE INSURRECTION
DURING A TERRIFIC TROPICAL
STORM, HE LED HIS MEN
ACROSS A RIVER THROUGH
A HAIL OF BULLETS TO THE
RESCUE OF OTHER TROOPS,
BRINGING THEM FOOD
AND AMMUNITION.

FOLLOWING IN THE FOOTSTEPS OF
THEIR FAMOUS PREDECESSOR— THESE CADETS
WERE RECENTLY COMMISSIONED IN THE U.S. ARMY.

Rather than promote Charles Young and place him in a position of authority over white soldiers, the army involuntarily retired him from active duty, ostensibly because of ill health. To prove his fitness for duty, he rode on horseback from his home in Wilberforce, Ohio, to Washington, D.C. The army, nevertheless, did not promote him to colonel until after he retired from service. In a speech he gave while serving as military attaché in Liberia, Young stated, "America is the land of my race's forced adoption . . . the house is none the less loved and cherished by me. In that house the love of liberty, of the highest freedom, and of independence and fair play for all men, and the love of all men as such without distinction of race, color, or condition, entered into my heart." Charles Young is buried in Arlington National Cemetery.

Company M, 1st Ohio Infantry, of the Ohio National Guard was headquartered in Batavia when it was called to active service on July 15, 1917. Ten men from the company were killed in action, and the Carey Davis VFW Post No. 180 in Georgetown was named after one of them. Another member of the unit, Henry Hiser of Higginsport, single-handedly captured a German machine gun and took 52 Germans prisoner.

Tank Day on May 8, 1918, was reported in the *Ripley Bee*: "News that a war tank would be here Wednesday brought a large crowd of people in from the country." However, many residents did not know the exhibition was happening until it was over, so it gave another performance, which was "something wonderful, it traveled over the dump pile near Cherry Street, smashing down trees, going over piles of dirt, up and down the bank without any trouble."

Harold Chambers Baird was born in Ripley in 1890 to a prominent Ripley family. At the age of 18, Baird was commissioned a lieutenant and assigned as an instructor in aviation aerobatics. After the outbreak of World War I, he was sent to Europe where, within six months, he shot down six German airplanes. After the war, Baird returned to Ripley, where he died in 1960.

The American Legion Post No. 394 in Russellville was named in honor of Walter Miller, shown here, who was killed while fighting in France during World War I. Since 1920, the post has assisted in many local and civic projects in Russellville and in Brown County.

During World War II, Howard "Shorty" Kabler of Ripley was at D-day plus five where he was wounded, spending almost a year in the hospital. Shorty was the Brown County veterans service officer for many years and held so many state positions in Veterans Affairs that they cannot be listed. He was instrumental in getting the Southern Ohio Veteran's Home built in Brown County in 2003.

Howard L. Kabler

During World War II, women had to do many of the men's jobs while the war was going on, and Brown County was no exception to that rule. Many women had to do the farming while their husbands, brothers, and sons were off fighting the war. In this photograph, taken in the Mary P. Shelton Library, ladies of Georgetown work for the Red Cross, rolling bandages.

"Most Remarkable Bird on Record". Trained Eagle "Brownie" after one year in captivity. Owned by C. A. White, Ripley, O.

C. A. WHITE, Saddlery, RIPLEY, O. (Formerly) Nicholasville, Ky.

Very little is known about this postcard, but it looked so interesting that it had to be included. The card says, "'Most Remarkable Bird on Record'. Trained Eagle 'Brownie' after one year in captivity. Owned by C. A. White, Ripley, O." And stamped on the right side it says, "C. A. White, Saddlery, Ripley, O. (Formerly) Nicholasville, Ky."

Legend has it that this tree house provided protection to the legendary Daniel Boone, who hid in its interior from Native Americans. In this photograph, the owner of the tree, F. F. Young, sits inside the doorway in 1903. This tree sat on the Young family property on South Street for many years.

This great photograph shows Main Street and Grant Avenue in Georgetown. Dunn's Corner, built in 1900 as a bank, later becoming Steele's Drugstore, is left of center with the turret on top. Other businesses on Main Street are the Corner Pharmacy, Work and Pobst Hardware, and Andrews and Fite Grocery.

Main St., Ripley, Ohio.

This postcard is of Ripley in 1908, looking north on Main Street. Notice the mud in the streets and all the carriages on both sides of the street. That is the Maddox Drug Company on the left at the corner of Main and Second Streets.

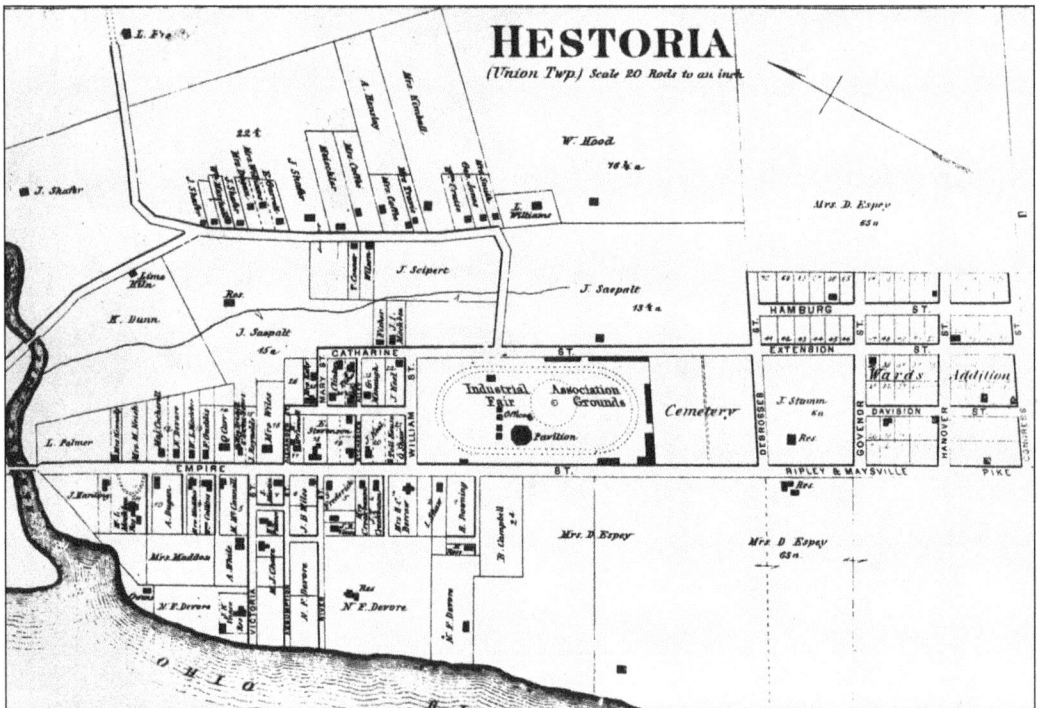

HESTORIA

(Union Twp.) Scale 20 Rods to an inch

East of the Red Oak Bridge, or the Second Street Bridge, was once called Hestoria. It was named in 1860 after the family of an early citizen of Ripley, Nicholas Devore. He put together the names of wife Hester and daughter Victoria to make the name in an attempt to lay out a new town. Hestoria was later annexed by Ripley.

The Mount Orab depot was built on land owned by the Cincinnati and Eastern Railroad in 1884. It is believed to be the oldest building in Mount Orab. For many years, the station handled passengers, freight, and mail. On Sunday, the station was packed with people going back to work for the week in Cincinnati. In October 1975, it was added to the list of the National Register of Historic Places.

The Ripley Progress Club held bake sales from 1910 to 1917 to collect money to build the Union Township Public Library. Andrew Carnegie also donated $10,000 for the building. The library was built above the 1913 flood level, but that did not stop the 1937 flood that destroyed many of the books. Today this library has branches in Aberdeen and Russellville.

The Mary P. Shelton Library building in Georgetown was a gift from Mary Cochran and named for her granddaughter. The library opened in 1924 and stands at the corner of Pleasant Street and Grant Avenue where the old National Union Hotel once stood. The Mary P. Shelton is the main branch of the Brown County Library System, which has three other libraries, Mount Orab, Sardinia, and Fayetteville.

Is this a Georgetown traffic jam of yesteryear? If one looks carefully at the center, toward the right of the photograph, one can see that there are no horses attached to the carriages in the street. Were they all in the H. L. Jennings Stable in the background? Perhaps everyone had gathered for Court Day, which was a day when court was in session, and onlookers were permitted in the courtroom.

This interesting Ripley photograph shows many sites that are not a part of the modern landscape. This is the intersection of Second Street and Market Street. Notice the tree-lined street; the trees were removed when the street was paved. The two houses next to the Methodist church are now gone, as is the church steeple. The water pump and the old theater on the left are also long gone.

On Main Street in the 400 block are three beautiful homes of the neoclassical period that were built during the antebellum period by Samuel Hemphill, Dr. Alexander Dunlap, and Charles Ridgeway, respectively. These three brick houses have had many famous visitors through the years; admirals, generals, and even presidents have paid a visit in these lovely homes.

Charles and Amalia Zaumseil lived at 422 Main Street in Ripley, where Charles also owned and operated a jewelry store for many years. They purchased this house in 1891 and moved their store from 12 Main Street to 426 Main Street at about the same time. He sold clocks, watches, fine jewelry, cutlery, and pistols from his store.

Greetings from Ripley, O.

Union School.

The Ripley Union School building was built in the 1860s and has served as a school, fire department, town hall, and jail, all at the same time. A town clock was added in 1869, purchased in New York for the cost of $650. This building was torn down in 1915 to be replaced by a new school building.

In 1932, Ripley High School was built with an auditorium and athletic field on the site of the old Ripley Fairgrounds. It served three generations of students. In 1956, Higginsport was added to the Ripley-Union School District to make it Ripley-Union-Lewis. This building was added on to in 1961. The building, which was beloved by many, was razed in 2005.

Front Street, Mt. Orab, Ohio   5385

Here are two views of Mount Orab from yesteryear. The photograph above is where U. S. 68 going north and Old Ohio 32, or the Cross County Highway, intersect. The lower shot is of the old public school. Today Mount Orab is one of the fastest-growing communities in Brown County and Ohio, with new retail establishments and businesses being added over the last several years.

As many readers may recall, before the President's Day holiday in February, many Americans celebrated George Washington's birthday on his actual birthday of February 22. This is the cast of the play "Reception at Mount Vernon," by first and second graders of Ripley in 1932, giving a performance in honor of Washington's birthday.

This is a wonderful class photograph because of who is not in it. Seen here are the classes of 1889 and 1890 in Ripley. Sarah Perry Stevenson should be in the next-to-the-last row on the right. Notice the black spot on the right end of the picture. She did not like her picture, so she asked the photographer to darken her face. Instead, he blotted out her face entirely.

Built in 1898, this was the second Georgetown Elementary School. When the Alverda Reed building opened in 1958, this building was closed as a school, although several citizens purchased the building, and today there are several shops located here. As this book is being published, the Alverda Reed School is being replaced by a brand-new building.

As the reader can tell, this is an integrated class at the old Georgetown Elementary School. It is a third-grade class at the school, and although the photograph is undated, it was probably taken in the early 1900s. Brown County was ahead of many of its neighbors when it came to race relations.

Russellville High School was built in 1910. This is what the school looked like in 1916. Later a new school was built that encompassed this building. Russellville High School was closed in 1962, and today it serves as the home of village offices, some small businesses, and the Russellville Museum.

In 1845, Julia Chatfield led a group of 11 Ursuline sisters from France to the northern tip of Brown County at St. Martins. Calling themselves the Ursulines of Brown County, they started the School of the Brown County Ursulines, a girls' boarding school that they operated until 1981. Chatfield College, also at St. Martins, was started by the sisters in 1971. The sisters also run the Ursuline Academy, which is located in Blue Ash, a Cincinnati suburb.

St. Michaels Church in Ripley was remodeled in 1971. It is shown in this photograph before that time. Notice the three altars, the two stained-glassed windows, the Blessed Virgin Mary on the left, and the Sacred Heart of Jesus on the right. The beautiful paintings were done between 1904 and 1922 by a German artist by the name of Brausch. In 1938, modern stained-glass windows, imported from Innsbruck, Austria, were installed.

The first Lutheran church in Arnheim was built in 1852, and the pastor gave the sermon in German for many years. In 1912, a new church, pictured here, was built. This church has beautiful art-glass windows, which were imported from Germany. In 1960, further additions were made to the church.

This church in Georgetown held court while the current county courthouse was being built in Georgetown. Hubbard Baker, who designed and built the courthouse, also built this church, the First Methodist, in 1847. The bell in this church actually came from the previous courthouse and was given to the church as a gift from the county commissioner. A fire destroyed this church in 1923, and a new church was built in 1929.

The Christian Church
Georgetown, Ohio

Perhaps the oldest congregation in Georgetown is the Christian Church, first organized in 1823. Its old building, pictured here, was dedicated in 1927. In 1991, the church moved to Hamer Road and is one of the largest churches in Brown County. Today this church is the New Beginnings Assembly of God.

The inside of St. Patrick's of Fayetteville was even more beautiful than the outside of the building. The cornerstone for this church was laid in 1837 by Bishop Purcell of Cincinnati. By 1904, St. Patrick's had 1,500 members. This early photograph shows a communion rail as well as angels to the right and left of the altar.

THE BATTALION. ST. ALOYSIUS MILITARY ACADEMY, FAYETTEVILLE, OHIO

The battalion of the old St. Aloysius Military Academy in Fayetteville is shown here in 1906. This building became a military boarding school in 1913 and closed in 1952, when there were 18 sisters and 104 students. The building was later used by an order of sisters, then an order of brothers. Today this building is Fayetteville-Perry High School.

The Ripley centennial parade of August 6, 1912, is shown in this photograph, with 14-year-old Gertrude Buchanan on the Trapp and Gardner float. Trapp and Gardner later became Trapp and Wilson, and it is still in business almost 100 years later but has moved to Maysville, Kentucky.

Please come to my party at the Fair Ground next Wednesday, Sept. 2, 1925 from Two to Five P. M.

Helen Reed Frank

Helen Roush was born in 1913 and was the daughter of Mary Helen Frank and George Frank of Ripley. George Frank was a Brown County commissioner, and for Helen's birthday, he threw her a party at the county fairgrounds. Mary Helen was very active in showing and judging horses in Ohio and Kentucky and very supportive of various charities in Brown and Adams Counties during her life.

Depending on how one counts it, this is the fourth or fifth building to be used as a courthouse in Brown County's history, but to many, this is the only real courthouse. In 1849, the county commissioners felt that the Brown County Courthouse was inadequate and employed Hubbard Baker, who was an architect and builder, to construct a new courthouse. While the courthouse was being built, the basement of the Methodist church, which is close to the courthouse square, was rented and used as a courtroom. The current courthouse was completed in 1851. Many sensational trials have been held in the courthouse, and many people in the past attended the trials as if going to a picnic, often finding that it was standing-room only. Additions were made to the courthouse in 1909. In 1977, a fire almost destroyed this structure, which was then restored. The courthouse remains in use today and is one of the oldest courthouses in Ohio still active.

Visit us at
arcadiapublishing.com